FOURTH EDITION

Perl
Pocket Reference

Johan Vromans

Beijing · Cambridge · Farnham · Köln · Paris · Sebastopol · Taipei · Tokyo

Perl Pocket Reference, Fourth Edition

by Johan Vromans

Copyright © 2002, 2000, 1998, 1996 Johan Vromans. All rights reserved.
Printed in the United States of America. Previous editions of this book were
published as *Perl 4 Pocket Reference* and *Perl 5 Pocket Reference*.

Published by O'Reilly Media, Inc., 1005 Gravenstein Highway North,
Sebastopol, CA 95472.

O'Reilly Media, Inc. books may be purchased for educational,
business, or sales promotional use. Online editions are also available
for most titles (*safari.oreilly.com*). For more information contact our
corporate/institutional sales department: (800) 998-9938 or
corporate@oreilly.com.

Editor:	Linda Mui
Cover Designer:	Hanna Dyer
Interior Designer:	Melanie Wang

Printing History:

February 1996:	First Edition.
August 1998:	Second Edition.
May 2000:	Third Edition.
July 2002:	Fourth Edition.

0-596-00374-9
[C]   [11/04]

Table of Contents

Perl Pocket Reference

The *Perl Pocket Reference* is a quick reference guide to Larry Wall's Perl programming language. It contains a concise description of all statements, functions, and variables, and lots of other useful information. This edition is based on Perl version 5.8.

The purpose of the Pocket Reference is to aid users of Perl in finding the syntax of specific functions and statements and the meaning of built-in variables. It is *not* a self-contained user guide; basic knowledge of the Perl language is required. It is also *not* complete; some of the more obscure variants of Perl constructs have been left out. But all functions and variables are mentioned in at least one way they can be used.

See Appendix B, *Perl Links*, on page 85 for more information on Perl resources.

Conventions

this	denotes text that you enter literally.
this	means variable text, i.e., things you must fill in.
this†	means that if *this* is omitted, $_ will be used instead.
word	is a keyword, i.e., a word with a special meaning.
[...]	denotes an optional part.
🕮	points to related documents, which can be viewed with a perldoc command.

Command-Line Options

--   Stops processing options.

-0 [*octnum*]

            (That's the number zero.) Designates an initial octal value for the record separator $/. See also -l below.

-a   Turns on autosplit mode when used with -n or -p. Splits to @F.

-c   Checks syntax but does not execute. It does run **BE-GIN** and **CHECK** blocks.

-C   Uses native wide-character system APIs, if supported by the system.

-d [:*module*]

            Runs the script under the indicated module. Default module is the Perl debugger. Use -de 0 to start the debugger without a script.

-D *flags* Sets debugging flags.

-e *commandline*

            May be used to enter a single line of script. Multiple -e commands may be given to build up a multiline script.

-F *pat*   Specifies a pattern on which to split if -a is in effect.

-h   Prints the Perl usage summary. Does not execute.

-i [*ext*]

            Activates in-place editing for files processed by the < > construct.

-I *dir*   The directory is prepended to the search path for Perl modules, @INC. Combined with -P, -I also tells the C preprocessor where to look for include files.

-l [*octnum*]

            (That's the letter el.) Enables automatic line ending processing, e.g., -l013.

-m[-]*module* [=*arg* [,*arg*...]]

            See -M on the facing page.

-M[-]*module* [=*arg* [,*arg...*]]

> Does a **use** *module* before executing the script. With - does a **no** *module* instead.

-n   Assumes an input loop around the script. Lines are not printed.

-p   Assumes an input loop around the script. Lines are printed.

-P   Runs the C preprocessor on the script before compilation by Perl.

-s   Interprets *-xxx* on the command line as a switch and sets the corresponding variable $*xxx* in the script to 1. If the switch is of the form *-xxx=yyy*, the $*xxx* variable is set to *yyy*.

-S   Uses the PATH environment variable to search for the script.

-t   Turns on *taint* checking. **warn**s on taint violations.

-T   Turns on *taint* checking. **die**s on taint violations.

-u   Dumps core after compiling the script. To be used with the *undump* program. Obsolete.

-U   Allows Perl to perform certain unsafe operations.

-v   Prints the version and patch level of your Perl executable. Does not execute anything.

-V [:*var*]

> Prints Perl configuration information, e.g., -V:man.dir. Does not execute anything.

-w   Prints warnings about possible spelling errors and other error-prone constructs in the script. Can be enabled and disabled under program control.

-W   Enables warnings permanently.

-x [*dir*] Extracts the program script from the input stream. If *dir* is specified, Perl switches to this directory before running the script.

-X   Disables warnings permanently.

Command-line options -D, -I, -M, -T, -U, -d, -m, t, and -w may also be specified using environment variable PERL5OPT. All options except -M and -m may be used on the #! line of the Perl script.

 perlrun.

Syntax

Perl is a free-format programming language. This means that in general it does not matter how a Perl program is written with regard to indentation and lines.

An exception to this rule is when the Perl compiler encounters a sharp or pound symbol (#) in the input: it then discards this symbol and everything following it up to the end of the current input line. This can be used to put comments in Perl programs. Real programmers put lots of useful comments in their programs.

There are places where whitespace does matter: within literal text, patterns, and formats.

If the Perl compiler encounters the special token __END__, it discards this symbol and stops reading input. Anything following this token is ignored by the Perl compiler, but can be read by the program when it is run, using the filehandle DATA.

When Perl is expecting a new statement and encounters a line that starts with =, it skips all input up to and including a line that starts with =cut. This is used to embed documentation.

 perlsyn.

Embedded Documentation

Tools exist to extract embedded documentation and generate input suitable for several formatters like troff, LaTeX, and HTML. The following commands can be used to control embedded documentation:

=back   See =over below.

=begin *fmt*

> Sets the subsequent text up to a matching =end to be included only when processed for formatter *fmt*.

=cut   Ends a document section.

=end *fmt*   See =begin.

=for *fmt*   Restricts the remainder of just this paragraph to be included only when processed for formatter *fmt*.

=head*N* *heading*

> Produces a heading. *N* must be 1, 2, 3, or 4.

=item *text*

> See =over below.

=over *N*   Starts an enumeration with indent *N*. Items are specified using =item. The enumeration is ended with =back.

=pod   Introduces a document section. Any of the = commands can be used to introduce a document section.

Each of the preceding commands applies to the paragraph of text that follows them; paragraphs are terminated by at least one empty line.

An indented paragraph is considered to be verbatim text and will be rendered as such.

Within normal paragraphs, markup sequences can be inserted:

B<*text*>   Bold text (for switches and programs).

C<*code*>   Literal code.

E<*escape*>

> A named character, e.g., E<lt> means a < and E<gt> means a >.

F<*file*>   Filename.

I<*text*>   Italic text (for emphasis and variables).

L< [*text* |] [*ref*] [/ *section*] >

> A cross reference. *text*, if present, is used for output.

S<*text*>   Text that cannot break on spaces.

X*<index>*
     An index entry.

Z< >   A zero-width character.

Markup sequences may be nested. If a markup sequence has to contain > characters, use C<< ... >> or C<<< ... >>>, etc. The last of the opening < *must* be followed by whitespace, and whitespace *must* precede the first of the closing >.

🔖 perlpod, perlpodspec.

Data Types

Array	Indexable list of scalar values.
Code	A piece of Perl code, e.g., a subroutine.
IO	Filehandle. Used in input and output operations.
Format	A format for producing reports.
Glob	All data types.
Hash	Associative array of scalar values.
Scalar	Strings, numbers, typeglobs, and references.

Perl variables can have a distinct value for each of these data types simultaneously.

🔖 perldata.

Quotes and Interpolation

Perl uses customary quotes to construct strings and such, but also implements a generic quoting mechanism. In the following table q// means that anything placed between the slashes is treated as if it were placed between single quotes, but it also means that you may use any nonalphanumeric, nonspace character instead of the slashes. Grouping characters like (), {}, [], and < > must be used in pairs.

When the quoting mechanism involves three delimiters you can also use two pairs of grouping characters, e.g., s{ ... }[...].

Customary	Generic	Meaning	Inter.	Page
`' '`	`q//`	Literal string	No	9
`" "`	`qq//`	Literal string	Yes	9
`` `` ``	`qx//`	Command execution	Yes	9
`()`	`qw//`	Word list	No	9
`//`	`m//`	Pattern match	Yes	37
`s///`	`s///`	Pattern substitution	Yes	38
`y///`	`tr///`	Character translation	No	38
`" "`	`qr//`	Regular expression	Yes	8

The "Inter." column of the table above indicates whether string escape sequences are interpolated. If single quotes are used as delimiters for pattern matching or substitution, no interpolation takes place.

String escape sequences:

\a	ASCII Alarm (bell).
\b	ASCII Backspace.
\e	ASCII Escape.
\f	ASCII Formfeed.
\n	ASCII Newline.
\r	ASCII Return.
\t	ASCII Tab.

Combining prefixes construct characters, for example:

\53   Interpreted as octal. This is an ASCII +. Octal escapes take up to three octal digits, including leading zeros. The resulting value must not exceed 377 octal.

In patterns, which are like **qq//** strings, leading zeros are mandatory in octal escapes to avoid interpretation as a back-reference unless the value exceeds the number of captures or 9, whichever is lower. Note that if it's a back-reference, the value is interpreted as decimal, not as octal.

\cC   Interpreted as a control character: Control-C.

`\N{BLACK SPADE SUIT}`
> A named character: ♠. This requires the charnames pragma; see page 21.

`\xeb`   Interpreted as hexidecimal: Latin-1 ë. Hex escapes take one or two hex digits.

`\x{03a3}` Unicode hexadecimal: Greek Σ.

These escape sequences change the meaning of what follows:

`\E`   Ends \L, \Q, and \U.

`\l`   Lowercases the following character.

`\L`   Lowercases up to a \E.

`\u`   Titlecases the following character.

`\U`   Uppercases until a \E is encountered.

`\Q`   Quotes nonword characters until \E.

▣ perlop, perlunicode, perluniintro.

Literal Values

Scalar Values

Array reference
```
[1,2,3]
```
Code reference
```
sub { statements }
```
Hash reference
```
{key1 => val1, key2 => val2, ... }
```
Equivalent to {key1, val1, key2, val2, ... } .

Numeric
```
123 1_234 123.4 5E-10 0b010101 (binary) 0xff (hex)
0377 (octal)
```
`__LINE__` (line number in the current program)

Regular Expression
```
qr/string/modifiers
```
See the section "("Regular Expressions) on page 32.

String

    'abc'

        Literal string, no variable interpolation or escape characters, except \' and \\.

    "abc"

        A string in which variables are interpolated and escape sequences are processed.

    `command`

        Evaluates to the output of the command.

    Class::

        A value that is mostly equivalent to "Class".

    1.2.3   v5.6.0.1

        A string ("v-string") composed of the specified ordinals. The ordinal values may be in the Unicode range. v1.3 is equivalent to "\x{1}\x{3}". Suitable to be compared to other v-strings using string compare operators.

    <<*identifier*

        Shell-style "here document."

    __FILE__

        The name of the program file.

    __PACKAGE__

        The name of the current package.

List Values

(...)   (1,2,3) is a list of three elements.

        (1,2,3)[0] is the first element from this list.

        (1,2,3)[-1] is the last element.

        ( ) is an empty list.

        (1..4) is the same as (1,2,3,4); likewise ('a'..'z').

        ('a'..'z')[4,7,9] is a slice of a literal list.

qw   qw/fo br.../ is the same as ('fo','br', ...).

< ... >   *<pattern>* evaluates to all filenames according to the C-shell wildcard pattern. Use <${*var*}> or glob $*var* (page 54) to glob from a variable.

Hash Values

(...)   (key1 => val1, key2 => val2,...)
        Equivalent to (key1, val1, key2, val2,...).

Filehandles

Predefined filehandles
        STDIN, STDOUT, STDERR, ARGV, DATA.
User-specified filehandles
        handle, $*var*.

Variables

$var   A simple scalar variable.

$p = \$var
        Now $p is a reference to scalar $var.

$$p   The scalar referenced by $p.

@var   An array. In scalar context, the number of elements in the array.

$var[6] Seventh element of array @var.

$var[-1]
        The last element of array @var.

$p = \@var
        Now $p is a reference to array @var.

$$p[6] or $p->[6]
        Seventh element of array referenced by $p.

${$p[6]}
        The scalar referenced by $p[6].

$p = \$var[6]
        Now $p is a reference to the seventh element of array @var.

$p = [1,3,'ape']
        Now $p is a reference to an anonymous array with three elements.

`$var[$i][$j]`

   $j-th element of $i-th element of array @var.

`$#var`   Last index of array @var .

`@var[3,4,5]`

   A slice of array @var.

`%var`   A hash. In scalar context, true if the hash has elements.

`$var{'red'}` or `$var{red}`

   A value from hash %var. The hash key may be specified without quotes if it is simple identifier.

`$p = \%var`

   Now $p is a reference to hash %var.

`$$p{'red'}` or `$p->{'red'}`

   A value from the hash referenced by $p.

`${$p{'red'}}`

   The scalar referenced by $p{'red'}.

`$p = {red => 1, blue => 2, yellow => 3}`

   Now $p is a reference to an anonymous hash with three elements.

`@var{'a','b'}`

   A slice of %var; same as ($var{'a'},$var{'b'}).

`$var{'a',1, ... }`

   Multidimensional hash (obsolete).

`$c = \&mysub`

   Now $c is a reference to subroutine mysub.

`&$c( `*args*` )` or `$c->( `*args*` )`

   A call to the subroutine via the reference.

`$c = sub { ... }`

   Now $c is a reference to an anonymous subroutine.

pkg::var

   A variable from a package, e.g., $pkg::var, @pkg::ary. The default package is main.

`*`*name*   Symbol table entry (typeglob). Refers to everything represented by *name*.

*n1{SCALAR} is the same as \$n1; *n1{ARRAY} is the same as \@n1. Other possibilities are HASH, CODE, GLOB, and IO.

Package variables can be aliased by assigning a reference to the typeglob:

> *n1 = \$n2 makes $n1 an alias for $n2.
> *n1 = *n2 makes all n1 aliases for n2.

Instead of the variable identifier, a *block* (see page 15) that returns the right type of reference can be used. For example, ${ $x > 0 ? \$y[4] : \$z }.

⛩ perldata, perlref.

Context

Perl expressions are always evaluated in a context that determines the outcome of the evaluation.

Boolean A special form of scalar context in which it only matters if the result is true or false. Anything that is undefined or evaluates to an empty string, the number zero, or the string "0" is considered false; everything else is true (including strings like "00").

List A list value is expected. Acceptable values are literal lists, arrays, and hashes. Slices of arrays, hashes, and lists are also acceptable. A scalar value will be interpreted as a one-argument list.

Scalar A single scalar value is expected.

Void No value is expected. If a value is provided, it is discarded.

The following functions relate to context:

scalar *expr*

> Forces scalar context for the expression.

wantarray

> Returns true in list context, false in scalar context, and *undef* in void context.

Operators and Precedence

Perl operators have the following associativity and precedence, listed from highest precedence to lowest. Table cells indicate groups of operators of equal precedence.

Assoc.	Operators	Description
right	terms and list operators	See below.
left	->	Infix dereference operator.
none	++ --	Auto-increment (magical on strings). Auto-decrement.
right	**	Exponentiation.
right right right	\ ! ~ + -	Reference to an object (unary). Unary negation, bitwise complement. Unary plus, minus.
left left	=~ !~	Binds a scalar expression to a pattern match. Same, but negates the result.
left	* / % x	Multiplication, division, modulo, repetition.
left	+ - .	Addition, subtraction, concatenation.
left	>> <<	Bitwise shift right, bitwise shift left.
right	named unary operators	E.g., **sin**, **chdir**, -f, -M.
none	< > <= >= **lt gt le ge**	Numerical relational operators. String relational operators.
none	== != <=> **eq ne cmp**	Numerical equal, not equal, compare. Stringwise equal, not equal, compare. Compare operators return −1 (less), 0 (equal), or 1 (greater).
left	&	Bitwise AND.
left	| ^	Bitwise OR, exclusive OR.
left	&&	Logical AND.
left	||	Logical OR.

↪

Assoc.	Operators	Description
none	`..`	Range operator.
	`...`	Alternative range operator.
right	`?:`	if ? then : else operator.
right	`=` `+=` `-=` etc.	Assignment operators.
left	`,`	Comma operator, also list element separator.
left	`=>`	Same, enforces the left operand to be a string.
right	list operators (rightward)	See below.
right	**not**	Low precedence logical NOT.
left	**and**	Low precedence logical AND.
left	**or**	Low precedence logical OR.
left	**xor**	Low precedence logical XOR.

Parentheses can be used to group an expression into a term.

A list consists of expressions, variables, arrays, hashes, slices, or lists, separated by commas. It will always be interpreted as one flat series of values.

Perl functions that can be used as list operators have either very high or very low precedence, depending on whether you look at the left side of the operator or at the right side of the operator. Parentheses can be added around the parameter lists to avoid precedence problems.

The logical operators do not evaluate the right operand if the result is already known after evaluation of the left operand.

🛈 perlop, perlfunc.
   perldoc -f *func* will provide extensive information on the named function.

Statements

A statement is an expression, optionally followed by a modifier, and terminated with a semicolon. Statements can be combined to form a *block* when enclosed in {}. The semicolon may be omitted after the last statement of a block.

Execution of expressions can depend on other expressions using one of the modifiers **if**, **unless**, **for**, **foreach**, **while**, or **until**, for example:

> *expr1* **if** *expr2* ;
> *expr1* **foreach** *list* ;

The operators **||**, **&&**, or **?:** also allow conditional execution, for example:

> *expr1* **||** *expr2* ;
> *expr1* **?** *expr2* **:** *expr3* ;

Blocks may be used for conditional execution:

> **if** (*expr*) *block* [[**elsif** (*expr*) *block* . . .] **else** *block*]
> **unless** (*expr*) *block* [**else** *block*]

Loop blocks:

> [*label*:] **while** (*expr*) *block* [**continue** *block*]
> [*label*:] **until** (*expr*) *block* [**continue** *block*]
> [*label*:] **for** ([*expr*] ; [*expr*] ; [*expr*]) *block*
> [*label*:] **foreach** *var*†(*list*) *block* [**continue** *block*]
> [*label*:] *block* [**continue** *block*]

In **foreach**, the iteration variable (default $_) is aliased to each element of the list, so modifying this variable modifies the actual list element.

The keywords **for** and **foreach** can be used interchangeably.

In loop blocks, program flow can be controlled with:

goto *label*

> Finds the statement labeled with *label* and resumes execution there. *label* may be an expression that evaluates to the name of a label.

last [*label*]

> Immediately exits the loop. Skips the **continue** block.

next [*label*]

> Executes the **continue** block and starts the next iteration of the loop.

redo [*label*]

> Restarts the loop block without evaluating the conditional again. Skips the **continue** block.

Special forms are:

> **do** *block* **while** *expr* ;
> **do** *block* **until** *expr* ;

which are guaranteed to perform *block* once before testing *expr*, and

> **do** *block*

which effectively turns *block* into an expression.

Subroutines

Subroutines need to be *declared*, i.e., specified how they should be called, and *defined*, i.e., specified what they should do when called.

sub *name* [(*proto*)] [*attributes*]

> Declares *name* as a subroutine, optionally specifying the prototype and attributes. Declaring a subroutine is optional, but allows the subroutine to be called just like Perl's built-in operators.

sub [*name*] [(*proto*)] [*attributes*] *block*

> Defines subroutine *name*, with optional prototype and attributes. If the subroutine has been declared with a prototype or attributes, the definition should have the same prototype and attributes. When *name* is omitted, the subroutine is anonymous and the definition returns a reference to the code.

When a subroutine is called, the statements in *block* are executed. Parameters are passed as a flat list of scalars as array @_. The elements of @_ are aliases for the scalar parameters. The call returns the value of the last expression evaluated. **wantarray** (page 12) can be used to determine the context in which the subroutine was called.

Subroutines that have an empty prototype and do nothing but return a fixed value are inlined, e.g., sub PI() { 3.1415 }.

attributes are introduced with a : (colon). The following attributes are currently implemented:

method The subroutine is a method.

locked Lock this subroutine against concurrent access.

lvalue The subroutine returns a variable that can be assigned to.

There are several ways to call a subroutine.

name ([*parameters*])

> The most common way. The parameters are passed by reference as array @_.

&*name* ([*parameters*])

> Prototype specifications, if any, are ignored.

&*name* The current @_ is passed directly to the called subroutine.

name [*arguments*]

> If the subroutine has been declared, or defined, it may be called as a built-in operator, without parentheses.

In all cases, *name* can be an expression yielding a reference to a code object. If so, you can also use &${*expr*}([*arguments*]) or ${*expr*}->([*arguments*]).

caller [*expr*]

> Returns a list (*package*, *file*, *line*, ...) for a specific subroutine call. caller returns this information for the current subroutine, caller(1) returns this information for the subroutine that called this subroutine, etc. Returns false if no caller.

defined &*name*

> Tests whether the named subroutine has been defined (has a body).

do *name list*

> Deprecated form of &*name*.

exists &*name*

> Tests whether the named subroutine has been declared, either in full (with a body) or with a forward declaration.

goto &*name*

> Substitutes a call to *name* for the current subroutine.

prototype *name*

> Returns the prototype for the named function as a string, or *undef* if the function has no usable prototype.

return [*expr*]

> Returns from a subroutine, **eval**, or **do** *file* with the value specified. Without *expr*, returns *undef* in scalar context and an empty list in list context.

Special Subroutines

Special subroutines are user defined, but are called by Perl while processing the program. They can be used to change the order in which parts of a program are executed.

[**sub**] **AUTOLOAD** *block*

> The code in *block* is executed when the program calls an undefined subroutine. $AUTOLOAD contains the name of the called subroutine, and @_ contains the parameters.

[**sub**] **BEGIN** *block*

> The code in *block* is executed immediately when compilation of the block is complete.

[**sub**] **CHECK** *block*

> **CHECK** blocks are executed in reverse order when the compilation of the program finishes.

[**sub**] **END** *block*

> **END** blocks are executed in reverse order when the Perl interpreter terminates. Inside the **END** blocks, $? contains the status with which the program is going to **exit**.

[**sub**] **INIT** *block*

> **INIT** blocks are executed immediately before the Perl interpreter starts executing the program.

📖 `perlsub`.

Packages and Modules

import *module* [*list*]

> Usually imports subroutines and variables from *module* into the current package. **import** is not a built-in, but an ordinary class method that may be inherited from UNIVERSAL.

no *module* [*list*]

> At compile time, **require**s the module and calls its **unimport** method on *list*. See **use** on the next page.

package [*namespace*]

> Designates the remainder of the current block or file as a package with a namespace. Omitting *namespace* is deprecated.

require *version*

> Requires Perl to be at least this version. *version* can be numeric like 5.005 or 5.008001, or a v-string like v5.8.1.

require *expr*†

> If *expr* is numeric, behaves like **require** *version*. Otherwise *expr* must be the name of a file that is included from the Perl library. Does not include more than once, and yields a fatal error if the file does not evaluate to true. If *expr* is a bare word, assumes extension .pm for the name of the file.

unimport *module* [*list*]

> Usually cancels the effects of a previous **import** or **use**. Like **import**, **unimport** is not a built-in, but an ordinary class method.

use *version*

> Requires Perl to be at least this version. *version* can be numeric like **5.005** or **5.008001**, or a v-string like **v5.8.0** or **5.8.1**.

use *module* [*version*] [*list*]

> At compile time, **require**s the module, optionally verifies the version, and calls its **import** method on *list*. Normally used to import a list of variables and subroutines from the named module into the current package.

🛛 perlmod.

Pragmatic Modules

Pragmatic modules affect the compilation of your program. Pragmatic modules can be activated (imported) with **use** and deactivated with **no**. These are usually lexically scoped.

attributes

> Enables attributes.

autouse *module* => *funcs*

> Determines that the module will not be loaded until one of the named functions is called.

base *classes*

> Establishes an IS-A relationship with the named classes at compile time.

bigint [*options*]

> Uses the Math::BigInt package to handle all integer calculations transparently.
>
> *options* can be **accuracy**, **precision**, **trace**, **version**, and **lib**. One-letter abbreviations are allowed. Accuracy and precision require a numeric argument, and lib requires the name of a Perl module to handle the calculations.

bignum [*options*]

> Uses the Math::BigNum package to handle all numeric

---

calculations transparently.

See `bigint` on the facing page for *options*.

bigrat Use the `Math::BigNum` and `Math::BigRat` packages to handle all numeric calculations transparently.

See `bigint` on the preceding page for *options*.

blib [*dir*]

Uses the MakeMaker's uninstalled version of a package. *dir* defaults to the current directory. Used for testing of uninstalled packages.

bytes Treat character data as strict 8-bit bytes, as opposed to Unicode UTF-8.

charnames [*sets*]

Enables character names to be expanded in strings using `\N` escapes.

constant *name* => *value*

Defines *name* to represent a constant value.

diagnostics [*verbosity*]

Forces verbose warning diagnostics and suppression of duplicate warnings. If *verbosity* is **-verbose**, makes it even more verbose.

encoding [*encoding*]
encoding *encoding* [`STDIN` => *inenc*] [`STDOUT` => *outenc*]

Sets the script encoding and pushes the *encoding* I/O layer for standard input and standard output. The second form allows you to select the I/O layers explicitly.

fields *names*

Implements compile-time verified class fields.

filetest [*strategy*]

Changes the way the file test operators (page 39) get their information. Standard strategy is **stat**, alternative is **access**.

if *condition* , *module* => *args*

`use`s a module if a condition holds.

integer Enables integer arithmetic instead of double precision floating point.

less *what*

    Requests less of something (unimplemented).

lib *names*

    Adds libraries to **@INC**, or removes them, at compile time.

locale   Uses POSIX locales for built-in operations.

open   Establishes default I/O layers for input and output.

ops *operations*

    Restricts unsafe operations when compiling.

overload *operator* => *subref*

    Overloads Perl operators. *operator* is the operator (as a string), *subref* a reference to the subroutine handling the overloaded operator.

re *behaviors*

    Alters regular expression behavior. *behaviors* can be any combination of **eval** (allows patterns to contain assertions that execute Perl code, even when the pattern contains interpolated variables; see page 34), **taint** (propagates tainting), **debug**, and **debugcolor** (produce debugging info).

sigtrap *info*

    Enables simple signal handling. *info* is a list of signals, e.g., **qw(SEGV TRAP)**.

sort [*options*]

    Controls **sort** behaviour. *options* can be **stable** to require stability, **_quicksort** (or **_qsort**) to use a quicksort algorithm, and **_mergesort** to use a merge-sort algorithm.

strict [*constructs*]

    Restricts unsafe constructs. *constructs* can be any combination of **refs** (restricts the use of symbolic references), **vars** (requires all variables to be either predefined by Perl, imported, global or lexical scoped, or fully qualified), and **subs** (restricts the use of bareword identifiers that are not subroutines).

---

subs *names*

> Predeclares subroutine names, allowing you to use them without parentheses even before they are declared.

threads Enables the use of interpreter-based threads. See the section "Threads" on on page 70.

threads::shared

> Adds data sharing between threads.

utf8 Enables or disables UTF-8 (or UTF-EBCDIC) in source code.

vars *names*

> Predeclares variable names, allowing you to use them even if they are not fully qualified under the strict pragma. Obsolete; use our (page 58) instead.

vmsish [*features*]

> Controls VMS-specific language features. VMS only. *features* can be any combination of exit (enables VMS-style exit codes), status (allows system commands to deliver VMS-style exit codes to the calling program), and time (makes all times relative to the local time zone).

warnings [*class*]

> Controls built-in warnings for classes of conditions.

warnings::register

> Creates a warnings category for the current package.

📖 perlmodlib.

Object-Oriented Programming

An *object* is a referent that knows which class it belongs to.

A *class* is a package that provides methods. If a package fails to provide a method, the base classes as listed in @ISA are searched, depth first.

A *method* is a subroutine that expects an invocant (an object reference or, for static methods, a package name) as the first argument.

bless *ref* [, *classname*]
> Turns the referent *ref* into an object in *classname* (default is the current package). Returns the reference.

invocant->method [(*parameters*)]
> Calls the named method.

method invocant [*parameters*]
> Provides an alternative way of calling a method, using the sometimes ambiguous *indirect object* syntax.

See also **ref** (page 58), and the next section.

🔁 perlobj, perlboot, perltoot, perltooc.

Special Classes

The special class UNIVERSAL contains methods that are automatically inherited by all other classes:

can *method*
> Returns a reference to the method if its invocant has it, *undef* otherwise.

isa *class* Returns true if its invocant is *class*, or any class inheriting from *class*.

VERSION [*need*]
> Returns the version of its invocant. Checks the version if *need* is supplied.

These methods can be used as normal functions as well, e.g., UNIVERSAL::isa($c,Math::Complex::).

The pseudopackage CORE provides access to all Perl built-in functions, even when they have been overridden.

The pseudopackage SUPER provides access to base class methods without having to specify which class defined that method. This is meaningful only when used inside a method.

Arithmetic Functions

abs *expr†*

> Returns the absolute value of its operand.

atan2 *y, x*

> Returns the arctangent of y/x in the range $-\frac{\pi}{2}$ to $+\frac{\pi}{2}$.

cos *expr†*

> Returns the cosine of *expr* (expressed in radians).

exp *expr†*

> Returns *e* to the power of *expr*.

int *expr†* Returns the integer portion of *expr*.

log *expr†*

> Returns the natural logarithm (base *e*) of *expr*.

not *expr* Logically negates the truth value of *expr*.

rand [*expr*]

> Returns a random fractional number between 0 (inclusive) and the value of *expr* (exclusive). If *expr* is omitted, it defaults to 1.

sin *expr†*

> Returns the sine of *expr* (expressed in radians).

sqrt *expr†*

> Returns the square root of *expr*.

srand [*expr*]

> Sets the random number seed for the **rand** operator.

time   Returns the number of non-leap seconds since whatever time the system considers to be the epoch. Suitable for feeding to **gmtime** and **localtime**.

Conversion Functions

chr *expr†*

> Returns the character represented by the decimal value *expr*.

gmtime [*expr*]

> In list context, converts a time as returned by the **time**

function to a nine-element list with the time localized for the standard Greenwich Mean Time (UTC, or Zulu).

In scalar context, returns a formatted string.

Use the standard module `Time::gmtime` for by-name access to the elements of the list; see **localtime** below.

hex *expr*†

Returns the decimal value of *expr* interpreted as an hexadecimal string. The string may, but need not, start with 0x. For other conversions, see **oct** below.

localtime [*expr*]

Like **gmtime**, but uses the local time zone.

Use the standard module `Time::localtime` for by-name access to the elements of the list:

Index	Name	Description
0	sec	Seconds.
1	min	Minutes.
2	hour	Hours.
3	mday	Day in the month.
4	mon	Month, 0 = January.
5	year	Years since 1900.
6	wday	Day in week, 0 = Sunday.
7	yday	Day in year, 0 = January 1st.
8	isdst	True during daylight savings time.

oct *expr*†

Returns the decimal value of *expr* interpreted as an octal string. If the string starts off with 0x, it will be interpreted as a hexadecimal string; if it starts off with 0b, it will be interpreted as a binary string.

ord *expr*†

Returns the ordinal value of the first character of *expr*.

vec *expr, offset, bits*

> Treats string *expr* as a vector of unsigned integers of *bits* bits each, and yields the decimal value of the element at *offset*. *bits* must be a power of 2 greater than 0. May be assigned to.

Structure Conversion

pack *template, list*

> Packs the values in *list* into a sequence of bytes, using the specified template. Returns this sequence as a string.

unpack *template, expr*

> Unpacks the sequence of bytes in *expr* into a list, using *template*.

template is a sequence of characters as follows:

a / A	Byte string, null-/space-padded
b / B	Bit string in ascending/descending order
c / C	Signed/unsigned byte value
d / D	Native double/long double
f / F	Native float/Perl internal float
h / H	Hex string, low/high nybble first
i / I	Signed/unsigned integer value
j / J	Perl internal integer/unsigned
l / L	Signed/unsigned long value
n / N	Short/long in network (big endian) byte order
p / P	Pointer to a null-terminated/fixed-length string
q / Q	Signed/unsigned quad value
s / S	Signed/unsigned short value
u / U	Uuencoded string/Unicode UTF-8 character code
v / V	Short/long in VAX (little endian) byte order
w	A BER compressed integer
x / X	Null byte (skip forward)/Back up a byte
Z / @	Null-terminated string/null fill to position

The size of an integer, as used by i and I, depends on the system architecture. Nybbles, bytes, shorts, longs, and quads are always exactly 4, 8, 16, 32, and 64 bits respectively. Characters s, S, l, and L may be followed by a ! to signify native shorts and longs instead. x and X may be followed by a ! to specify alignment.

Each character, or group of characters between parentheses, may be followed by a decimal number, optionally between [and], that will be used as a repeat count; an asterisk (*) specifies all remaining arguments. A template between [and] is a repeat count equal to the length of the packed template.

Starting the template with U0 forces the result to be Unicode UTF-8, C0 forces bytes.

If a format is preceded with %*n*, **unpack** returns an *n*-bit checksum instead. *n* defaults to 16.

Whitespace may be included in the template for readability, and a # character may be used to introduce comments.

A special case is a numeric character code followed by a slash and a string character code, e.g., C/a. Here the numeric value determines the length of the string item.

q and Q are only available if Perl has been built with 64-bit support. D is only available if Perl has been built to support long doubles.

▣ perlpacktut.

String Functions

chomp *list†*

>Removes $/ (page 64) from all elements of the list; returns the (total) number of characters removed.

chop *list†*

>Chops off the last character on all elements of the list; returns the last chopped character.

crypt *plaintext, salt*

>Encrypts a string (irreversibly).

eval *expr*†

Parses and executes *expr* as if it were a Perl program. The value returned is the value of the last expression evaluated. If there is a syntax error or runtime error, *undef* is returned by **eval**, and $@ is set to the error message. See also **eval** on page 58.

index *str*, *substr* [, *offset*]

Returns the position of *substr* in *str* at or after *offset*. If the substring is not found, returns −1.

lc *expr*†   Returns a lowercase version of *expr*. See also \L on page 8.

lcfirst *expr*†

Returns *expr* with its first character in lowercase. See also \l on page 8.

length *expr*†

Returns the length in characters of *expr*.

quotemeta *expr*†

Returns *expr* with all regular expression metacharacters quoted. See also \Q on page 8.

rindex *str*, *substr* [, *offset*]

Returns the position of the last *substr* in *str* at or before *offset*. If the substring is not found, returns −1.

substr *expr*, *offset* [, *len* [, *newtext*]]

Extracts a substring of length *len* starting at *offset* out of *expr* and returns it. If *offset* is negative, counts from the end of the string. If *len* is negative, leaves that many characters off the end of the string. Replaces the substring with *newtext* if specified. Otherwise, may be assigned to.

uc *expr*†   Returns an uppercase version of *expr*. See also \U on page 8.

ucfirst *expr*†

Returns *expr* with its first character titlecased. See also \u on page 8.

Array and Hash Functions

defined *expr*†

> Not specifically an array or hash function, but provides a convenient way to test whether an array or hash element has a defined value.

delete *lku*
delete @*array*[*index1*, ...]
delete @*hash*{*key1*, *key2*, ... }

> *lku* must be an array lookup like $*array*[*index*] or *expr*->[*index*], or a hash key lookup like $*hash*{*key*} or *expr*->{*key*}. Deletes the specified elements from the array or hash. Returns aliases to the deleted values. Deleting the last element(s) of an array will shorten the array.

each %*hash*

> In list context, returns a two-element list consisting of the key and an alias to the value for the next element of the hash. In scalar context, returns only the key. Entries are returned in an apparently random order. After all values of the hash have been returned, an empty list is returned. The next call to **each** after that will start iterating again. A call to **keys** or **values** will reset the iteration.

exists *lku*

> *lku* must be an array a hash lookup (see **delete** above). Checks whether the specified array element or hash key exists.

grep *expr*, *list*
grep *block* *list*

> Evaluates *expr* or *block* for each element of the list, locally aliasing $_ to the element. In list context, returns the list of elements from *list* for which *expr* or *block* returned true. In scalar context, returns the number of such elements.

---

join *expr, list*

    Returns the string formed by inserting *expr* between all elements of *list* and concatenating the result.

keys *%hash*

    In list context, returns a list of all the keys of the named hash. In scalar context, returns the number of elements of the hash. Can be assigned to, to pre-extend the hash.

map *expr, list*
map *block list*

    Evaluates *expr* or *block* for each element of the list, locally aliasing $_ to the element. Returns the list of results.

pop [*@array*]

    Pops off and returns the last value of the array. If *@array* is omitted, pops @_ if inside a subroutine; otherwise pops @ARGV.

push *@array, list*

    Pushes the values of the list onto the end of the array. Returns the length of the resulting array.

reverse *list*

    In list context, returns the list in reverse order. In scalar context, concatenates the list elements and returns the reverse of the resulting string.

scalar *@array*

    Returns the number of elements in the array.

scalar *%hash*

    Returns true if there are keys in the hash.

shift [*@array*]

    Shifts the first value of the array off and returns it, shortening the array by 1 and moving everything down. If *@array* is omitted, shifts @_ if inside a subroutine; otherwise shifts @ARGV.

sort [*subroutine*] *list*

    Sorts the *list* and returns the sorted list value. *subroutine*, if specified, must return less than zero, zero, or greater than zero, depending on how the elements of the list are to be ordered.

subroutine may be the name of a user-defined routine, a variable containing that name, or a *block*. If the subroutine has been declared with a prototype of (\$\$), the values to be compared are passed as normal parameters; otherwise, they are available to the routine as package global variables \$a and \$b.

splice @*array*, *offset* [, *length* [, *list*]]

Removes the elements of @*array* designated by *offset* and *length*, and replaces them with *list* (if specified). Returns the elements removed. If *offset* is negative, counts from the end of the array.

split [*pattern* [, *expr*† [, *limit*]]]

Uses *pattern* to split *expr* (a string) into a list of strings, and returns it. If *limit* is a positive number, splits into at most that number of fields. A negative value indicates the maximum number of fields. If *limit* is omitted, or 0, trailing empty fields are not returned. If *pattern* is omitted, splits at the whitespace (after skipping any leading whitespace). If not in list context, returns number of fields and splits to @_.

unshift @*array*, *list*

Prepends *list* to the front of the array. Returns the length of the resultant array.

values %*hash*

Returns a list consisting of aliases to all the values of the named hash.

Regular Expressions

Each character matches itself, unless it is one of the special characters +?.*^\$()[{|\. The special meaning of these characters can be escaped using a \.

The *multiline* and *single-line* modes are discussed in the section "Search and Replace Functions" on on page 37.

.   Matches any character, but not a newline. In single-line mode, matches newlines as well.

(...)   Groups a series of pattern elements to a single element. The text the group matches is captured for later use. It is also assigned immediately to $^N to be used during the match, e.g., in a (?{ ... }).

^   Matches the beginning of the target. In multiline mode, also matches after every newline character.

$ Matches the end of the line, or before a final newline character. In multiline mode, also matches before *every* newline character.

[...]   Denotes a class of characters to match. [^ ...] negates the class.

... | ... | ...

            Matches the alternatives from left to right, until one succeeds.

(?# *text*)

            Comment.

(? [*modifier*] : *pattern*)

            Acts like (*pattern*) but does not capture the text it matches. *modifier* can be one or more of i, m, s, or x. Modifiers can be switched off by preceding the letter(s) with a minus sign, e.g., si-xm. See page 37 for the meaning of the modifiers.

(?= *pattern*)

            Zero-width positive look-ahead assertion.

(?! *pattern*)

            Zero-width negative look-ahead assertion.

(?<= *pattern*)

            Zero-width positive look-behind assertion.

(?<! *pattern*)

            Zero-width negative look-behind assertion.

(?{ *code* })

> Executes Perl code while matching. Always succeeds with zero width. Can be used as the condition in a conditional pattern selection. If not, the result of executing *code* is stored in $^R.

(??{ *code* })

> Executes Perl code while matching. Interprets the result as a pattern.

(?> *pattern*)

> Like (?: *pattern*), but prevents backtracking inside.

(?(*cond*) *ptrue* [| *pfalse*])

> Selects a pattern depending on the condition. *cond* should be the number of a parenthesized subpattern, or one of the zero-width look-ahead, look-behind, and evaluate assertions.

(? *modifier*)

> Embedded pattern-match modifier. *modifier* can be one or more of i, m, s, or x. Modifiers can be switched off by preceding the letter(s) with a minus sign, e.g., (?si-xm).

Quantified subpatterns match as many times as possible. When followed with a ? they match the minimum number of times. These are the quantifiers:

+
> Matches the preceding pattern element one or more times.

?
> Matches zero or one times.

*
> Matches zero or more times.

{*n*,*m*}
> Denotes the minimum *n* and maximum *m* match count. {*n*} means exactly *n* times; {*n*,} means at least *n* times.

Patterns are processed as double-quoted strings, so standard string escapes have their usual meaning (see page 7). An exception is \b, which matches word boundaries, except in a character class, where it denotes a backspace again.

A \ escapes any special meaning of nonalphanumeric characters, but it turns most alphanumeric characters into something special:

\1 ... \9   Refer to matched subexpressions, grouped with (). \10 and up can also be used if the pattern has that many subexpressions.

\w   Matches alphanumeric plus _. \W matches non-\w.

\s   Matches whitespace. \S matches nonwhitespace.

\d   Matches numeric. \D matches nonnumeric.

\A   Matches the beginning of the string.

\Z   Matches the end of the string or before a newline at the end of the string.

\z   Matches the physical end of the string.

\b   Matches word boundaries. \B matches nonboundaries.

\G   Matches where the previous search with a **g** modifier left off.

\p*p*   Matches a named property. \P*p* matches non-*p*. Use \p{*prop*} for names longer than one single character.

\X   Matches extended Unicode combining character sequence.

\C   Matches a single 8-bit byte.

\1 and up, \d, \D, \p, \P, \s, \S, \w, and \W may be used inside and outside character classes.

POSIX classes are used inside character classes, like [[:alpha:]]. These are the POSIX classes and their Unicode property names:

[:alpha:] \p{IsAlpha}
          Matches one alphabetic character.

[:alnum:] \p{IsAlnum}
          Matches one alphanumeric character.

[:ascii:] \p{IsASCII}
          Matches one ASCII character.

[:blank:] \p{IsSpace}
          Matches one whitespace character, almost like \s.

`[:cntrl:]` `\p{IsCntrl}`
>   Matches one control character.

`[:digit:]` `\p{IsDigit}`
>   Matches one numeric character, like `\d`.

`[:graph:]` `\p{IsGraph}`
>   Matches one alphanumeric or punctuation character.

`[:lower:]` `\p{IsLower}`
>   Matches one lowercase character.

`[:print:]` `\p{IsPrint}`
>   Matches one alphanumeric or punctuation character
>   or space character.

`[:punct:]` `\p{IsPunct}`
>   Matches one punctuation character.

`[:space:]` `\p{IsSpace}`
>   Matches one whitespace character, almost like `\s`.

`[:upper:]` `\p{IsUpper}`
>   Matches one uppercase character.

`[:word:]` `\p{IsWord}`
>   Matches one word character, like `\w`.

`[:xdigit:]` `\p{IsXDigit}`
>   Matches one hexadecimal digit.

In general, the "Is" prefix may be omitted for property names.

The equivalent of `\s` is `\p{IsSpacePerl}`.

The POSIX classes can be negated with a `^`, e.g., `[:^print:]`, the named properties by using `\P`, e.g., `\P{IsPrint}`.

See also `$1 ... $9`, `$+`, `` $` ``, `$&`, `$'`, `$^R`, and `$^N` on page 67, and `@-` and `@+` on page 68.

With modifier x, whitespace and comments can be embedded in the patterns.

Regular expression patterns can be compiled and used as values with the **qr** quoting operator: **qr**/*string*/*modifiers* compiles *string* as a pattern according to the (optional) modifiers, and returns the compiled pattern as a scalar value.

📖 perlre, perlretut, perlrequick, perlunicode.

Search and Replace Functions

[*expr* =~] [**m**] /*pattern*/ [**g** [**c**]] [**i**] [**m**] [**o**] [**s**] [**x**]

Searches *expr* (default $_) for a pattern.

For =~, its negation !~ may be used, which is true when =~ would return false, and vice versa.

After a successful match, the following special variables are set:

$&   The string that matched.
$`   The string preceding what was matched.
$'   The string following what was matched.
$1   The first parenthesized subexpression that matched, $2 the second, and so on.
$+   The last subexpression that matched.
@-   The start offsets of the match and submatches.
@+   The corresponding end offsets.

If used in list context, a list is returned consisting of the subexpressions matched by the parentheses in pattern, i.e., ($1,$2,$3, . . .).

Optional modifiers are:

c   (with **g**) prepares for continuation.
g   matches as many times as possible.
i   searches in a case-insensitive manner.
o   interpolates variables only once.
m   treats the string as multiple lines. ^ and $ will match at embedded newline characters.
s   treats the string as a single line. . will match embedded newline characters.
x   allows for whitespace and comments.

If *pattern* is empty, the most recent pattern from a previous successful **m//** or **s///** is used.

With **g**, the match in scalar context can be used as an iterator. The iterator is reset upon failure, unless **c** is also supplied.

See page 6 for generic quoting rules and string interpolation.

?*pattern*?

> This is just like the /*pattern*/ search, except that it matches only once between calls to the **reset** operator.

[$*var* =~] **s**/*pattern*/*newtext*/ [e] [g] [i] [m] [o] [s] [x]

> Searches the string *var* (default $_) for a pattern, and if found, replaces that part with the replacement text.
>
> If successful, sets the special variables as described with **m//** and returns the number of substitutions made. Otherwise, it returns false.
>
> Optional modifiers are:
>
> g   replaces all occurrences of the pattern.
> e   evaluates *newtext* as a Perl expression.
>
> For the other modifiers, see **m**/*pattern*/ matching on the page before.
>
> If *pattern* is empty, the most recent pattern from a previous successful **m//** or **s///** is used.
>
> See page 6 for generic quoting rules and string interpolation.

[$*var* =~] **tr**/*search*/*replacement*/ [c] [d] [s]

> Transliterates all occurrences of the characters found in the search list into the corresponding character in the replacement list. It returns the number of characters replaced.
>
> Optional modifiers are:
>
> c   complements the search list.
> d   deletes all characters found in the search list that do not have a corresponding character in the replacement list.
> s   squeezes all sequences of characters that are translated into the same target character into one occurrence of this character.
>
> See page 6 for generic quoting rules and string interpolation.

[$*var* =~] **y**/*search*/*replacement*/*modifiers*

> Identical to **tr**.

If the righthand side of the =~ or !~ is an expression rather than a search pattern, substitution, or transliteration, and its value is not the result of a **qr** operator, it is interpreted as a string and compiled into a search pattern at runtime.

pos *scalar*†

> Returns the position where the last /g search in *scalar* left off. Alters the location of \G if assigned to.

study *scalar*†

> Studies the scalar in anticipation of performing many pattern matches on its contents before the variable is next modified.

File Test Operators

These unary operators take one argument, either a filename or a filehandle, and test the associated file to see if something is true about it. If the argument is omitted, they test $_ (except for -t, which tests STDIN). If the special argument _ (underscore) is passed, they use the information from the preceding test or **stat** call.

See also the filetest pragma on page 21.

-r -w -x	File is readable/writable/executable by effective uid/gid.
-R -W -X	File is readable/writable/executable by real uid/gid.
-o -O	File is owned by effective/real uid.
-e -z	File exists/has zero size.
-s	File exists and has non-zero size. Returns the size.
-f -d	File is a plain file/a directory.
-l -S -p	File is a symbolic link/a socket/a named pipe (FIFO).
-b -c	File is a block/character special file.
-u -g -k	File has setuid/setgid/sticky bit set.
-t	Filehandle (default STDIN) is opened to a tty.
-T -B	File is a text/non-text (binary) file. These tests return true on an empty file, or a file at EOF when testing a filehandle.

-M -A -C   Returns the modification/access/inode-change time of the file. The value is relative to the time the program started and expressed in fractional days. See also `$^T` on page 66.

File Operations

Functions operating on a list of files return the number of files successfully operated upon.

chmod *list*

Changes the permissions of a list of files. The first element of the list must be the numerical mode. If this is a number, it must be in octal, e.g., `0644`.

chown *list*

Changes the owner and group of a list of files. The first two elements of the list must be the numerical user id and group id. If either is −1, that property is not changed.

link *oldfile, newfile*

Creates a new filename linked to the old file.

lstat *file†*

Like **stat**, but if the last component of the filename is a symbolic link, **stat**s the link instead of the file it links to. *file* can be an expression evaluating to a filename, or _ to refer to the last file test -1 operation or **lstat** call.

mkdir *dir* [*, perm*]

Creates a directory with permissions specified by *perm* and modified by the current umask. If *perm* is a number, it must be an octal number. Default value for *perm* is `0777`. See also **umask** on page 55.

readlink *expr†*

Returns the name of the file pointed to by the symbolic link designated by *expr*.

rename *oldname, newname*

Changes the name of a file.

rmdir *expr†*

Deletes the directory if it is empty.

stat *file†* Returns a 13-element list with file information. *file* can be a filehandle, an expression evaluating to a filename, or _ to refer to the last file test operation or **stat** call. Returns an empty list if the **stat** fails.

Use the standard module File::stat for by-name access to the elements of the list:

Index	Name	Description
0	dev	Device code.
1	ino	Inode number.
2	mode	Type and access flags.
3	nlink	Number of hard links.
4	uid	User id of owner.
5	gid	Group id of owner.
6	rdev	Device type.
7	size	Size, in bytes.
8	atime	Timestamp of last access.
9	mtime	Timestamp of last modification.
10	ctime	Timestamp of last status change.
11	blksize	File system block size.
12	blocks	Size, in blocks.

symlink *oldfile, newfile*

Creates a new filename symbolically linked to the old filename.

truncate *file, size*

Truncates *file* to *size*. *file* may be a filename or a file-handle.

unlink *list*†

> Deletes a list of files.

utime *list*

> Changes the access and modification times. The first two elements of the list must be the numerical access and modification times. When both elements are *undef*, the current time is used.

> The inode change time will be set to the current time.

Input and Output

In input/output operations, *filehandle* may be a filehandle as opened by the **open** operator, a predefined filehandle (e.g., STDOUT), or a scalar variable that evaluates to a reference to or the name of a filehandle to be used.

⟨*filehandle*⟩

> In scalar context, reads a single record, usually a line, from the file opened on *filehandle*. In list context, reads the rest of the file.

⟨ ⟩

⟨ARGV⟩ Reads from the input stream formed by the files specified in @ARGV, or standard input if no arguments were supplied.

binmode *filehandle* [, *layers*]

> Arranges for the file opened on *filehandle* to be read or written using the specified I/O layers (default: :raw). For a list of standard I/O layers, see page 48.

close [*filehandle*]

> Closes the filehandle. Resets $. if it was an input file. If *filehandle* is omitted, closes the currently selected filehandle.

dbmclose %*hash*

> Closes the file associated with the hash. Superseded by **untie**, see page 51.

---

dbmopen %*hash, dbmname, mode*

Opens a dbm file and associates it with the hash. Superseded by **tie**, see page 51.

eof *filehandle*

Returns true if the next read will return EOF (end of file) or if the file is not open.

eof   Returns the EOF status for the last file read.

eof()   Indicates EOF on the pseudo-file formed of the files listed on the command line.

fcntl *filehandle, function, $var*

Calls system-dependent file control functions.

fileno *filehandle*

Returns the file descriptor for a given (open) file.

flock *filehandle, operation*

Calls a system-dependent locking routine on the file. *operation* is formed by adding one or more values or LOCK_ constants from the table on page 47.

getc [*filehandle*]

Returns the next character from the file, or an empty string on end of file. If *filehandle* is omitted, reads from STDIN.

ioctl *filehandle, function, $var*

Calls system-dependent I/O control functions.

open *filehandle* [, *modeandname*]
open *filehandle, mode, name* [, ...]

Opens a file and associates it with *filehandle*. If *filehandle* is an uninitialized scalar variable, a new, unique filehandle is automatically created.

modeandname must contain the name of the file, prefixed with the mode with which to open it. If *modeandname* is not provided, a global (package) variable with the same name as *filehandle* must provide the mode and name.

See page 46 for general open modes.

In *modeandname*, - may be used to designate standard input or output. Whitespace is allowed, as a consequence this form of **open** cannot easily be used to open files with names that start or end with whitespace.

The form with three or more arguments allows more control over the open mode and file name.

If *name* is **undef**, an anonymous temporary file is opened. If *name* is a reference to a scalar, the contents of the scalar are read from or written to.

mode may have a list of I/O layers appended that will be applied to the handle. For a list of standard I/O layers, see page 48.

pipe *readhandle, writehandle*

Creates a pair of connected pipes. If either handle is an uninitialized scalar variable, a new, unique filehandle is automatically created.

print [*filehandle*] *list*†

Prints the elements of *list*, converting them to strings if needed. If *filehandle* is omitted, prints to the currently selected output handle.

printf [*filehandle*] *list*†

Equivalent to **print** *filehandle* **sprintf** *list*.

read *filehandle, $var, length* [, *offset*]

Reads *length* characters from the file into the variable at *offset*. Returns the number of characters actually read, 0 on EOF, and *undef* on failure.

readline *expr*

Internal function that implements the < > operator.

readpipe *scalar expr*

Internal function that implements the **qx** operator. *expr* is executed as a system command.

seek *filehandle, position, whence*

Arbitrarily positions the file on a byte position. *whence* can be one of the values or SEEK_ constants from the table on page 47.

---

select [*filehandle*]

> Sets the current default filehandle for output operations if *filehandle* is supplied. Returns the currently selected filehandle.

select *rbits, wbits, nbits, timeout*

> Performs a *select* syscall with the same parameters.

sprintf *format, list*

> Returns a string resulting from formatting a (possibly empty) list of values. See the section "Formatted Printing" on page 48 for a complete list of format conversions. See the section "Formats" on page 50 for an alternative way to obtain formatted output.

sysopen *filehandle, path, mode* [, *perms*]

> Performs an *open* syscall. The possible values and flag bits of *mode* and *perms* are system-dependent; they are available via the standard module Fcntl. If *filehandle* is an uninitialized scalar variable, a new, unique filehandle is automatically created.
>
> *mode* is formed by adding one or more values or O_ constants from the table on page 47.

sysread *filehandle, $var, length* [, *offset*]

> Reads *length* characters into $var at *offset*. Returns the number of characters actually read, 0 on EOF, and *undef* on failure.

sysseek *filehandle, position, whence*

> Arbitrarily positions the file on a byte position, for use with **sysread** and **syswrite**. *whence* can be one of the values or SEEK_ constants from the table on page 47.

syswrite *filehandle, scalar* [, *length* [, *offset*]]

> Writes *length* characters from *scalar* at *offset*. Returns the number of characters actually written, or *undef* if there was an error.

tell [*filehandle*]

> Returns the current byte position for the file. If *filehandle* is omitted, assumes the file last read.

Open Modes

The following modes are valid for all forms of **open**:

<	Input only. This is the default when the mode is empty.
>	Output only. The file is created or truncated if necessary.
>>	Open the file in append mode. The file is created if necessary.
+<	Read/write update access.
+>	Write/read update access.
+>>	Read/append access.

These modes may be followed by & to duplicate an already opened filehandle or, if numeric, file descriptor. Use &= with a numeric argument to create an alias to the already opened file descriptor.

Modes for the two-argument **open** include:

|	Opens a pipe to read from or write to a command.
|-	Forks, with the file connected to the standard input of the child.
-|	Forks, with the file connected to the standard output of the child.

Modes for the three-argument **open** include:

|-	Opens a pipe to write to a command.
-|	Opens a pipe to read from a command.

📖 perlopentut.

Common constants

Several input/output related constants can be imported from the standard module Fcntl.

Constants related to **open** and **sysopen** are imported by default. For some constants, the widely accepted values are shown in octal.

Value	Name	Description
00000	O_RDONLY	Read-only access.
00001	O_WRONLY	Write-only access.
00002	O_RDWR	Read and write access.
00100	O_CREAT	Create the file if nonexistent.
00200	O_EXCL	Fail if the file already exists.
02000	O_APPEND	Append data to the end of the file.
01000	O_TRUNC	Truncate the file.
	O_NONBLOCK	Nonblocking input/output.
	O_NDELAY	Same as O_NONBLOCK.
	O_SYNC	Synchronous input/output.
	O_EXLOCK	Lock exclusive.
	O_SHLOCK	Lock shared.
	O_DIRECTORY	File must be a directory.
	O_NOFOLLOW	Do not follow symlinks.
	O_BINARY	Use binary mode for input/output.
	O_LARGEFILE	Allow file to be larger than 4 GB.
	O_NOCTTY	Terminal will not become the controlling tty.

Constants related to **seek** and **sysseek** must be imported explictly by specifying :seek in the import list of Fcntl.

Value	Name	Description
00	SEEK_SET	Seek position.
01	SEEK_CUR	Seek offset from current position.
02	SEEK_END	Seek offset from end of file.

Constants related to **flock** must be imported explictly by specifying :flock in the import list of Fcntl.

Value	Name	Description
001	LOCK_SH	Shared lock.
002	LOCK_EX	Exclusive lock.
004	LOCK_NB	Non-blocking lock.
010	LOCK_UN	Unlock.

Standard I/O Layers

:bytes   Use 8-bit bytes, as opposed to :utf8.

:crlf   Do CR/LF to newline translation, and vice versa.

:encoding(*enc*)
> Select a specific encoding.

:perlio   Use Perl's "PerlIO" implementation.

:raw   Use low-level I/O.

:stdio   Use the system's "standard I/O" implementation.

:unix   Use Unix-style low-level I/O.

:utf8   Use Perl's internal encoding of Unicode.

:Via(*module*)
> Use the specified module to handle the I/O.

:win32   Use native I/O (Microsoft Windows platforms only).

🄘 PerlIO, perlrun (under ENVIRONMENT/PERLIO).

Formatted Printing

printf and **sprintf** format a list of values according to a format string that may use the following conversions:

%%   A percent sign.

%b   An unsigned number (binary).

%c   The character corresponding to the ordinal value.

%d   A signed integer.

%e   A floating-point number (scientific notation).

%f   A floating-point number (fixed decimal notation).

%g   A floating-point number (%e or %f notation).

`%i`	A synonym for `%d`.
`%n`	The number of characters formatted so far is stored into the corresponding variable in the parameter list.
`%o`	An unsigned integer, in octal.
`%p`	A pointer (address in hexadecimal).
`%s`	A string.
`%u`	An unsigned integer (decimal).
`%x`	An unsigned integer (hexadecimal).
`%D`	An obsolete synonym for `%ld`.
`%E`	Like `%e`, but using an uppercase `E`.
`%F`	An obsolete synonym for `%f`.
`%G`	Like `%g`, but with an uppercase `E` (if applicable).
`%O`	An obsolete synonym for `%lo`.
`%U`	An obsolete synonym for `%lu`.
`%X`	Like `%x`, but using uppercase letters.

The following flags can be put between the `%` and the conversion letter:

space	Prefix a positive number with a space.
`+`	Prefix a positive number with a plus sign.
`-`	Left-align within the field.
`0`	Use zeroes instead of spaces to right-align.
`#`	With `o`, `b`, `x`, and `X`: prefix a nonzero number with `0`, `0b`, `0x`, or `0X`.
number	Minimum field width.
.number	For a floating-point number, the number of digits after the decimal point. For a string, the maximum length. For an integer, the minimum width.
`h`	Interpret integer as short or unsigned short according to the C type.
`l`	Interpret integer as long or unsigned long according to the C type.
`ll, L, q`	Interpret integer as quad (64-bit).
`v`	Print string as series of ordinals. Use with `d`, `o`, `b`, `x`, or `X`.
`V`	Interpret integer according to Perl's type.

An asterisk (*) may be used instead of a number; the value of the next item in the list will be used. With %*v, the next item in the list will be used to separate the values.

Parameter ordering can be obtained by inserting *n*$ directly after a % or *. This conversion will then use the *n*th argument from the list.

See the section "Formats" below for an alternative way to obtain formatted output.

Formats

formline *picture, list*
> Formats *list* according to *picture* and accumulates the result into $^A.

write [*filehandle*]
> Writes a formatted record to the specified file, using the format associated with that file. If *filehandle* is omitted, the currently selected one is taken.

Formats are defined as follows:

> **format** [*name*] =
> *formlist*
> .

formlist is a sequence of lines, each of which is either a comment line (# in the first column), a picture line, or an argument line. A picture line contains descriptions of fields. It can also contain other text that will be output as given. Argument lines contain lists of values that are output in the format and order of the preceding picture line.

name defaults to STDOUT if omitted.

To associate a format with the current output stream, assign its name to the special variable $~. A format to handle page breaks can be assigned to $^. To force a page break on the next **write**, set $- to zero.

Picture fields are:

@<<<   Left-adjusted field. Repeat the < to denote the desired width.

@>>>   Right-adjusted field.

@||| Centered field.

@##.##   Numeric format with implied decimal point.

@0#.##   Same, padded with leading zeros if necessary.

@*   Multiline field.

Use ^ instead of @ for multiline block filling.

Use ~ in a picture line to suppress unwanted empty lines.

Use ~~ in a picture line to have this format line repeated until it would yield a completely blank line. Use with ^ fields to have them repeated until exhausted.

See also $^, $~, $^A, $%, $:, $^L, $-, and $= in the section "Special Variables" on page 63.

🔖 perlform.

Tying Variables

tie *var, classname,* [*list*]

Ties a variable to a class that will handle it. *list* is passed to the class constructor.

tied *var*   Returns a reference to the object underlying *var*, or *undef* if *var* is not tied to a class.

untie *var*

Breaks the binding between the variable and the class. Calls an UNTIE method if provided.

A class implementing a tied scalar should define the methods TIESCALAR, DESTROY, FETCH, and STORE.

A class implementing a tied ordinary array should define the methods TIEARRAY, CLEAR, DESTROY, EXTEND, FETCHSIZE, FETCH, POP, PUSH, SHIFT, SPLICE, STORESIZE, STORE, and UNSHIFT.

A class implementing a tied hash should define the methods TIEHASH, CLEAR, DELETE, DESTROY, EXISTS, FETCH, FIRSTKEY, NEXTKEY, and STORE.

A class implementing a tied filehandle should define the methods TIEHANDLE, CLOSE, DESTROY, GETC, PRINTF, PRINT, READLINE, READ, and WRITE.

Several base classes to implement tied variables are available in the standard libraries: Tie::Array, Tie::Handle, Tie::Hash, Tie::RefHash, and Tie::Scalar.

▣ perltie.

Directory Reading Routines

closedir *dirhandle*
> Closes a directory opened by **opendir**.

opendir *dirhandle, dirname*
> Opens a directory on the handle specified. If *dirhandle* is an uninitialized scalar variable, a new, unique handle is automatically created.

readdir *dirhandle*
> In scalar context, returns the next entry from the directory or *undef* if none remains. The entry is the name component within the directory, not the full name.
>
> In list context, returns a list of all remaining entries from the directory.

rewinddir *dirhandle*
> Positions the directory at the beginning.

seekdir *dirhandle, pos*
> Sets the position for **readdir** on the directory. *pos* should be a file offset as returned by **telldir**.

telldir *dirhandle*
> Returns the position in the directory.

System Interaction

alarm *expr*†

Schedules a SIGALRM signal to be delivered after *expr* seconds. If *expr* is zero, cancels a pending timer.

chdir [*expr*]

Changes the working directory. Uses $ENV{HOME} or $ENV{LOGNAME} if *expr* is omitted.

chroot *filename*†

Changes the root directory for the process and any future children.

die [*list*]

Prints the value of *list* to STDERR and exits with value $! || ($? >> 8) || 255. *list* defaults to Died.

Inside an **eval**, the error message is stuffed into $@, and the **eval** is terminated returning *undef*; this makes **die** the way to raise an exception.

exec [*program*] *list*

Executes the system command in *list*; does not return. *program* can be used to explictly designate the program to execute the command.

exit [*expr*]

Exits immediately with the value of *expr*, which defaults to zero. Calls **END** routines and object destructors before exiting.

fork　　Does a *fork* syscall. Returns the process id of the child to the parent process (or *undef* on failure) and zero to the child process.

getlogin　Returns the current login name as known by the system. If it returns false, use **getpwuid**.

getpgrp [*pid*]

Returns the process group for process *pid*. If *pid* is zero, or omitted, uses the current process.

getppid　Returns the process id of the parent process.

getpriority *which, who*

> Returns the current priority for a process, process group, or user. Use `getpriority 0,0` to designate the current process.

glob *expr*†

> Returns a list of filenames that match the C-shell pattern(s) in *expr*. Use `File::Glob` for more detailed globbing control.

kill *list*   Sends a signal to a list of processes. The first element of the list must be the signal to send, either numerically (e.g., 1), or its name as a string (e.g., `HUP`). Negative signals affect process groups instead of processes.

setpgrp *pid, pgrp*

> Sets the process group for the *pid*. If *pid* is zero, affects the current process.

setpriority *which, who, priority*

> Sets the current priority for a process, process group, or a user.

sleep [*expr*]

> Causes the program to sleep for *expr* seconds, or forever if *expr* is omitted. Returns the number of seconds actually slept.

syscall *list*

> Calls the syscall specified in the first element of the list, passing the rest of the list as arguments to the call. Returns −1 (and sets $!) on error.

system [*program*] *list*

> Like **exec**, except that a fork is performed first, and the parent process waits for the child process to complete. During the wait, the signals `SIGINT` and `SIGQUIT` are passed to the child process.
>
> Returns the exit status of the child process. Zero indicates success, not failure.
>
> *program* can be used to explicitly designate the program to execute the command.

times   Returns a four-element list (user, system, cuser, csystem) giving the user and system times, in seconds, for this process and the children of this process.

umask [*expr*]

Sets the umask for the process and returns the old one. If *expr* is a number, it must be an octal number. If *expr* is omitted, **umask** does not change the current umask value.

wait   Waits for a child process to terminate and returns the process id of the deceased process (−1 if none). The status is returned in $?.

waitpid *pid, flags*

Performs the same function as the corresponding syscall. Returns 1 when process *pid* is dead, −1 if nonexistent.

warn [*list*]

Prints the *list* on STDERR like **die**, but doesn't exit. *list* defaults to Warning: something's wrong.

Networking

accept *newsocket, listeningsocket*

Accepts a new socket. If *newsocket* is an uninitialized scalar variable, a new, unique handle is automatically created.

bind *socket, name*

Binds the name to the socket.

connect *socket, name*

Connects a socket to the named peer.

getpeername *socket*

Returns the socket address of the other end of the socket.

getsockname *socket*

Returns the name of the socket.

getsockopt *socket, level, optname*
> Returns the socket options.

listen *socket, queuesize*
> Starts listening on the specified socket, allowing *queuesize* connections.

recv *socket, $var, length, flags*
> Receives a message of *length* characters on the socket and puts it into scalar variable *$var*.

send *socket, msg, flags* [*, to*]
> Sends a message on the socket.

setsockopt *socket, level, optname, optval*
> Sets the requested socket option.

shutdown *socket, how*
> Shuts the socket down.

socket *socket, domain, type, protocol*
> Creates a socket in the domain with the given type and protocol. If *socket* is an uninitialized scalar variable, a new, unique handle is created.

socketpair *socket1, socket2, domain, type, protocol*
> Works the same as **socket**, but creates a pair of bidirectional sockets.

System V IPC

use the standard module IPC::SysV to access the message- and semaphore-specific operation names.

msgctl *id, cmd, args*
> Calls *msgctl*. If *cmd* is IPC_STAT then *args* must be a scalar variable.

msgget *key, flags*
> Creates a message queue for *key*. Returns the message queue identifier.

msgrcv *id, $var, size, type, flags*
> Receives a message from queue *id* into *$var*.

msgsnd *id, msg, flags*

Sends *msg* to queue *id*.

semctl *id, semnum, cmd, arg*

Calls *semctl*. If *cmd* is IPC_STAT or GETALL then *arg* must be a scalar variable.

semget *key, nsems, size, flags*

Creates a set of semaphores for *key*. Returns the message semaphore identifier.

semop *key, ...*

Performs semaphore operations.

shmctl *id, cmd, arg*

Calls *shmctl*. If *cmd* is IPC_STAT then *arg* must be a scalar variable.

shmget *key, size, flags*

Creates shared memory. Returns the shared memory segment identifier.

shmread *id, $var, pos, size*

Reads at most *size* bytes of the contents of shared memory segment *id* starting at offset *pos* into *$var*.

shmwrite *id, string, pos, size*

Writes at most *size* bytes of *string* into the contents of shared memory segment *id* at offset *pos*.

▣ perlipc.

Miscellaneous

defined *expr*†

Tests whether the scalar expression has an actual value.

do { *expr* ; ... }

Executes the block and returns the value of the last expression. See also the section "Statements" on page 14.

do *filename*

Executes *filename* as a Perl script. See also **require** on page 19.

eval { *expr* ; ... }

> Executes the code between { and }. Traps runtime errors and returns as described with **eval**(*expr*) on page 29.

local [**our**] *variable*

> Gives a temporary value to the named package variable, which lasts until the enclosing block, file, or **eval** exits. *variable* may be a scalar, an array, a hash, or an element (or slice) of an array or hash.

my *variable*

> Creates a scope for the variable lexically local to the enclosing block, file, or **eval**.

my [*class*] *variable* [*attributes*]

> Experimental. Built-in attribute is `:shared`. Module `Attribute::Handlers` can be used to define additional attributes.

our *variable*

> Declares the variable to be a valid global within the enclosing block, file, or **eval**.

our [*class*] *variable* [*attributes*]

> Experimental. Built-in attributes are `:shared` and `:unique`. Module `Attribute::Handlers` can be used to define additional attributes.

ref *expr*†

> Returns true if *expr* is a reference. Returns the package name if *expr* has been blessed into a package.

reset [*expr*]

> *expr* is a string of single letters. All variables in the current package beginning with one of those letters are reset to their pristine state. If *expr* is omitted, resets ?? searches so that they work again.

undef [*lvalue*]

> Undefines the *lvalue*. Always returns *undef*.

Information from System Databases

Information About Users

In list context, each of these routines returns a list of values. Use the standard module User::pwent for by-name access to the elements of the list:

Index	Name	Description
0	name	User name
1	passwd	Password info
2	uid	Id of this user
3	gid	Group id of this user
4	quota	Quota information
5	comment	Comments
6	gecos	Full name
7	dir	Home directory
8	shell	Login shell
9	expire	Password expiration info

endpwent

> Ends lookup processing.

getpwent

> Gets next user information. In scalar context, returns the username.

getpwnam *name*

> Gets information by name. In scalar context, returns the user id.

getpwuid *uid*

> Gets information by user id. In scalar context, returns the username.

setpwent

> Resets lookup processing.

Information About Groups

In list context, each of these routines returns a list of values. Use the standard module User::grent for by-name access to the elements of the list:

Index	Name	Description
0	name	Group name
1	passwd	Password info
2	gid	Id of this group
3	members	Space-separated list of the login names of the group members

endgrent Ends lookup processing.

getgrent Gets next group information. In scalar context, returns the group name.

getgrgid *gid*
    Gets information by group id. In scalar context, returns the group name.

getgrnam *name*
    Gets information by name. In scalar context, returns the group id.

setgrent Resets lookup processing.

Information About Networks

In list context, each of these routines returns a list of values. Use the standard module Net::netent for by-name access:

Index	Name	Description
0	name	Network name
1	aliases	Alias names
2	addrtype	Address type
3	net	Network address

endnetent

Ends lookup processing.

getnetbyaddr *addr, type*

Gets information by address and type. In scalar context, returns the network name.

getnetbyname *name*

Gets information by network name. In scalar context, returns the network number.

getnetent

Gets next network information. In scalar context, returns the network name.

setnetent *stayopen*

Resets lookup processing.

Information About Network Hosts

In list context, each of these routines returns a list of values. Use the standard module `Net::hostent` for by-name access to the elements of the list:

Index	Name	Description
0	name	Host name
1	aliases	Alias names
2	addrtype	Address type
3	length	Length of address
4	addr	Address, or addresses

endhostent

Ends lookup processing.

gethostbyaddr *addr, addrtype*

Gets information by IP address. In scalar context, returns the hostname.

gethostbyname *name*

Gets information by hostname. In scalar context, returns the host address.

gethostent

> Gets next host information. In scalar context, returns the hostname.

sethostent *stayopen*

> Resets lookup processing.

Information About Network Services

In list context, each of these routines returns a list of values. Use the standard module Net::servent for by-name access to the elements of the list:

Index	Name	Description
0	name	Service name
1	aliases	Alias names
2	port	Port number
3	proto	Protocol number

endservent

> Ends lookup processing.

getservbyname *name, protocol*

> Gets information by service name for the given protocol. In scalar context, returns the service (port) number.

getservbyport *port, protocol*

> Gets information by service port for the given protocol. In scalar context, returns the service name.

getservent

> Gets next service information. In scalar context, returns the service name.

setservent *stayopen*

> Resets lookup processing.

Information About Network Protocols

In list context, each of these routines returns a list of values. Use the standard module `Net::protoent` for by-name access to the elements of the list:

Index	Name	Description
0	name	Protocol name
1	aliases	Alias names
2	proto	Protocol number

endprotoent
> Ends lookup processing.

getprotobyname *name*
> Gets information by protocol name. In scalar context, returns the protocol number.

getprotobynumber *number*
> Gets information by protocol number. In scalar context, returns the name of the protocol.

getprotoent
> Gets next protocol information. In scalar context, returns the name of the protocol.

setprotoent *stayopen*
> Resets lookup processing.

Special Variables

The alternative names for special variables are provided by the standard module `English`.

The following variables are global and should be localized in subroutines:

$_   Alternative: $ARG.
> The default input, output, and pattern-searching space.

$.	Alternatives: $INPUT_LINE_NUMBER, $NR.
	The current input line number of the last filehandle that was read. Reset only when the filehandle is closed explicitly.
$/	Alternatives: $INPUT_RECORD_SEPARATOR, $RS.
	The string that separates input records. Default value is a newline.
$,	Alternatives: $OUTPUT_FIELD_SEPARATOR, $OFS.
	The output field separator for the print functions. Default value is an empty string.
$"	Alternative: $LIST_SEPARATOR.
	The separator that joins elements of arrays interpolated in strings. Default value is a single space.
$\	Alternatives: $OUTPUT_RECORD_SEPARATOR, $ORS.
	The output record separator for the print functions. Default value is an empty string.
$#	The output format for printed numbers. Deprecated. Use **printf** instead.
$*	Set to 1 to do multiline matching within strings. Deprecated; see the m and s modifiers on page 37.
$?	Alternative: $CHILD_ERROR.
	The status returned by the last ` ... ` command, pipe **close**, **wait**, **waitpid**, or **system** function.
$]	The Perl version number, e.g., **5.006**. See also $^V on page 66.
$[	The index of the first element in an array or list, and of the first character in a substring. Default is zero. Deprecated. Do not use.
$;	Alternatives: $SUBSCRIPT_SEPARATOR, $SUBSEP.
	The subscript separator for multidimensional hash emulation. Default is "\034".
$!	Alternatives: $OS_ERROR, $ERRNO.
	If used in numeric context, yields the current value of **errno**. Otherwise, yields the corresponding error string.

| $@ | Alternative: $EVAL_ERROR. |
| | The Perl error message from the last **eval** or **do** *expr* command. |

| $: | Alternative: $FORMAT_LINE_BREAK_CHARACTERS. |
| | The set of characters after which a string may be broken to fill continuation fields (starting with ^) in a format. |

| $0 | Alternative: $PROGRAM_NAME. |
| | The name of the file containing the Perl script being executed. May be assigned to. |

| $$ | Alternatives: $PROCESS_ID, $PID. |
| | The process id of the Perl interpreter running this script. Altered (in the child process) by **fork**. |

| $< | Alternatives: $REAL_USER_ID, $UID. |
| | The real user id of this process. |

| $> | Alternatives: $EFFECTIVE_USER_ID, $EUID. |
| | The effective user id of this process. |

| $(| Alternatives: $REAL_GROUP_ID, $GID. |
| | The real group id of this process. |

| $) | Alternatives: $EFFECTIVE_GROUP_ID, $EGID. |
| | The effective group id, or a space-separated list of group ids, of this process. |

| $^A | Alternative: $ACCUMULATOR. |
| | The accumulator for **formline** and **write** operations. |

| $^C | Alternative: $COMPILING. |
| | True if Perl is run in compile-only mode using command-line option -c. |

| $^D | Alternative: $DEBUGGING. |
| | The debug flags as passed to Perl using command-line option -D. |

| $^E | Alternative: $EXTENDED_OS_ERROR. |
| | Operating-system dependent error information. |

| $^F | Alternative: $SYSTEM_FD_MAX. |
| | The highest system file descriptor, ordinarily 2. |

| $^H | The current state of syntax checks. |

$^I	Alternative: $INPLACE_EDIT. In-place edit extension as specified using command-line option -i.
$^L	Alternative: $FORMAT_FORMFEED. Formfeed character used in formats.
$^M	Emergency memory pool.
$^O	Alternative: $OSNAME. Operating system name.
$^P	Alternative: $PERLDB. Internal debugging flag.
$^S	Alternative: $EXCEPTIONS_BEING_CAUGHT. Current state of the Perl interpreter.
$^T	Alternative: $BASETIME. The time (as delivered by **time**) when the program started. This value is used by the file test operators -M, -A, and -C.
$^{TAINT}	The current state of taint mode.
$^V	Alternative: $PERL_VERSION. The Perl version as a v-string, e.g., 5.6.0. Use %vd format to print it.
$^W	Alternative: $WARNING. The value of the -w option as passed to Perl.
$^X	Alternative: $EXECUTABLE_NAME. The name by which Perl was invoked.
$AUTOLOAD	The name of the undefined subroutine that was called.

The following variables are context dependent and need not be localized:

$%	Alternative: $FORMAT_PAGE_NUMBER. The current page number of the currently selected output handle.
$=	Alternative: $FORMAT_LINES_PER_PAGE. The page length of the current output handle. Default is 60 lines.

| $- | Alternative: $FORMAT_LINES_LEFT. |
| | The number of lines remaining on the page. |

$-   Alternative: $FORMAT_LINES_LEFT.
        The number of lines remaining on the page.

$~   Alternative: $FORMAT_NAME.
        The name of the current report format.

$^   Alternative: $FORMAT_TOP_NAME.
        The name of the current top-of-page format.

$| Alternative: $OUTPUT_AUTOFLUSH.
        If set to nonzero, forces a flush after every write or
        print on the currently selected output handle. Default
        is zero.

$ARGV   The name of the current file when reading from < > .

The following variables are always local to the current block:

$&   Alternative: $MATCH.
        The string matched by the last successful pattern
        match.

$`   Alternative: $PREMATCH.
        The string preceding what was matched by the last
        successful match.

$'   Alternative: $POSTMATCH.
        The string following what was matched by the last
        successful match.

$+   Alternative: $LAST_PAREN_MATCH.
        The last bracket matched by the last search pattern.

$1 . . . $9 . . .
        Contain the subpatterns from the corresponding sets
        of parentheses in the last pattern successfully matched.
        $10 and up are only available if the match contained
        that many subpatterns.

$^N   Alternative: $LAST_SUBMATCH_RESULT.
        The text matched by the most recently closed group.

$^R   Alternative: $LAST_REGEXP_CODE_RESULT.
        Result of last (?{ *code* }).

▣ perlvar.

Special Arrays

The alternative names are provided by the standard module English.

@_   Alternative: @ARG.
          Parameter array for subroutines. Also used by **split** if not in list context.

@-   Alternative: @LAST_MATCH_START.
          After a successful pattern match, contains the offsets of the beginnings of the successful submatches. $-[0] is the offset of the entire match.

@+   Alternative: @LAST_MATCH_END.
          Like @-, but the offsets point to the ends of the sub-matches. $+[0] is the offset of the end of the entire match.

@ARGV   Contains the command-line arguments for the script (not including the command name, which is in $0).

@EXPORT   Names the methods and other symbols a package exports by default. Used by the Exporter module.

@EXPORT_OK
          Names the methods and other symbols a package can export upon explicit request. Used by the Exporter module.

@F   When command-line option -a is used, contains the split of the input lines.

@INC   Contains the list of places to look for Perl scripts to be evaluated by the **do** *filename*, **use** and **require** commands.
          Do not modify @INC directly, but use the lib pragma or -I command-line option instead.

@ISA   List of base classes of a package.

⚠ perlvar.

Special Hashes

%!   Requires the **Errno** module. Each element of %! has
            a nonzero value only if $! is set to that value.

%ENV   Contains the current environment. The key is the
            name of an environment variable; the value is its
            current setting.

%EXPORT_TAGS

            Defines names for sets of symbols. Used by the
            Exporter module.

%INC   Contains the list of files that have been included with
            use, **require**, or **do**. The key is the filename as spec-
            ified with the command; the value is the location of
            the file.

%SIG   Registers signal handlers for various signals. The
            key is the name of the signal (without the SIG
            prefix); the value a subroutine that is executed when
            the signal occurs.

            __WARN__ and __DIE__ are pseudo-signals to attach
            handlers to Perl warnings and exceptions.

▣ perlvar.

Environment Variables

Perl uses the following environment variables. This does not
include the environment variables used by library packages.

HOME   Used if **chdir** has no argument.

LC_ALL, LC_CTYPE, LC_COLLATE, LC_NUMERIC,
PERL_BADLANG, LANGUAGE, LANG

            Controls how Perl handles data specific to particular
            natural languages.

LOGDIR   Used if **chdir** has no argument and HOME is not set.

PATH   Used in executing subprocesses, and in finding the
            Perl script if -S is used.

PERL5LIB

> A colon-separated list of directories to search for Perl library files before looking in the standard library and the current directory.

PERL5DB The command to get the debugger code.

PERL_ENCODING

> Used by use encoding without an explicit encoding name.

PERLIO A space- or colon-separated list of I/O layers. This list becomes the default for all I/O operations.

PERLLIB Used instead of PERL5LIB if PERL5LIB is not defined.

PERL5OPT

> Initial (command-line) options for Perl.

PERL5SHELL

> The shell that Perl must use internally for executing system commands. Microsoft ports only.

Threads

Support for threads needs to be built into the Perl executable.

The pragma **threads** implements thread objects and the necessary operations for threads:

async *block*

> Starts a thread to execute the block. Returns the thread object.

threads->list

> Returns a list of joinable threads.

threads->new(*sub* [, *args*])

> Creates a new thread that starts executing in the referenced subroutine. The args are passed to this subroutine. Returns the thread object.

threads->self

> Returns an object representing the current thread.

`threads->yield`

> The current thread gives up the CPU in favor of other threads.

`thread` objects support the following methods:

detach   Detaches a thread so it runs independently.

equal(*thread*)

> Returns true if the thread and *thread* are the same thread. You can also compare thread objects directly, using the == operator.

join   Waits for the thread to complete. The value returned is the return value from the thread's subroutine.

tid   Returns the thread id of a thread.

The pragma `threads::shared` implements operations that enable variable sharing across threads:

cond_broadcast *variable*

> Unblocks all threads waiting for this variable. *variable* must be locked.

cond_signal *variable*

> Unblocks one thread that is waiting for this variable. *variable* must be locked.

cond_wait *variable*

> Waits for another thread to issue a **cond_signal** or **cond_broadcast** on the variable. *variable* must be locked and will be temporarily unlocked while waiting.

lock *variable*

> Locks a shared variable against concurrent access. The lock is automatically released when it goes out of scope.

share *variable*

> Marks the variable as shared.

𝌆 perlthrtut.

Compiler Backends

To compile a Perl program foo.pl with the C backend, use:

```
perlcc -o foo foo.pl
```

To produce a cross-reference report of the line numbers at which all variables, subroutines, and formats are defined and used, use:

```
perl -MO=Xref,-d foo.pl
```

To see what Perl compiles your program into, use:

```
perl -MO=Deparse foo.pl
```

This shows exactly the precedence of Perl operators:

```
perl -MO=Deparse,-p foo.pl
```

The compiler backends are experimental.

🔁 perlcc, perlcompile.

The Perl Debugger

The Perl symbolic debugger is invoked with perl -d.

Any input to the debugger that is not one of the commands enumerated below is evaluated as a Perl expression.

a [*line*] *command*
> Sets an action for *line*.

A [*line*] Deletes the action at the given line; default is the current line. If *line* is *, deletes all line actions.

b [*line* [*condition*]]
> Sets a breakpoint at *line*; default is the current line.

b *subname* [*condition*]
> Sets a breakpoint at the named subroutine.

b compile *subname*
> Stops after the subroutine is compiled.

b load *file*
> Sets a breakpoint at **require**ing the given file.

b postpone *subname* [*condition*]

Sets a breakpoint at the first line of the subroutine after it is compiled.

B [*line*] Deletes the breakpoint at the given line; default is the current line. If *line* is *, deletes all breakpoints.

c [*line*] Continues (until *line*, or another breakpoint, or exit).

f *file* Switches to *file* and starts listing it.

h Prints out a long help message.

h *cmd* Prints out help for debugger command *cmd*.

h h Prints out a concise help message.

H [*-number*]

Displays the last *-number* commands.

l [*range*]

Lists a range of lines. *range* may be a number, *start* - *end*, *start* + *amount*, or a subroutine name. If *range* is omitted, lists the next screenful.

l *subname*

Lists the named subroutine.

L [a|b|w]

Lists lines with actions, breakpoints, or watches.

m *class* Prints the methods callable via the given class.

m *expr* Evaluates the expression in list context, prints the methods callable on the first element of the result.

man [*topic*]

Views system documentation.

M Shows versions of loaded modules.

n [*expr*]

Single steps around the subroutine call.

o [*opt* [= *val*]]

Sets values of debugger options. Default value is true.

o *opt* ? Queries values of debugger options.

p *expr*† Evaluates *expr* in list context and prints the result. See also x on the next page.

q Quits the debugger. An end of file condition on the debugger input will also quit.

r	Returns from the current subroutine.
R	Restarts the debugger.
s [*expr*]	
	Single steps.
source *file*	
	Executes the debugger commands in the named file.
S [!] *pattern*	
	Lists the names of all subroutines [not] matching the pattern.
t	Toggles trace mode.
t *expr*	Traces through execution of *expr*.
T	Prints a stack trace.
v [*line*]	Lists a screenful of lines around the specified line.
V [*package* [*pattern*]]	
	Lists variables matching *pattern* in a package. Default package is main.
w *expr*	Adds a global watch-expression.
W [*expr*]	
	Deletes the global watch-expression. If *expr* is *, deletes all watch-expressions.
x *expr*	Evaluates *expr* in list context and dumps the result.
X [*pattern*]	
	Like V, but assumes the current package.
y [*n* [*pattern*]]	
	Like V, but lists lexicals in higher scope *n*. Requires the optional module PadWalker.
.	Returns to the executed line.
-	Lists the previous screenful of lines.
= [*alias* [*value*]]	
	Sets or queries an alias, or lists the current aliases.
/*pattern* [/]	
	Searches forward for *pattern*.
?*pattern* [?]	
	Searches backward for *pattern*.

< command

Sets an action to be executed before every debugger prompt. If *command* is ?, lists current actions.

<< command

Adds an action to the list of actions to be executed before every debugger prompt.

> command

Sets an action to be executed after every debugger prompt. If *command* is ?, lists current actions.

>> command

Adds an action to the list of actions to be executed after every debugger prompt.

{ command

Defines a debugger command to run before each prompt. If *command* is ?, lists current commands.

{{ command

Adds a debugger command to the list of debugger commands to run before each prompt.

! [[-] number]

Re-executes a command. Default is the previous command.

! [pattern]

Re-executes the last command that started with *pattern*.

!! [command]

Runs *command* in a sub-process.

| cmd   Runs debugger command *cmd* through the current pager.

|| cmd   Same as |*cmd*, but **selects** DB::OUT as well.

Pressing the Enter or Return key at the debugger prompt will repeat the last s or n command.

The debugger uses environment variables DISPLAY, EMACS, LESS, MANPATH, PERL5DB, PAGER, OS2_SHELL, SHELL, TERM and WINDOWID, as well as several other variables all starting with PERLDB_.

🔁 perldebug, perldebtut.

Appendix A: Standard Modules

These modules come standard with Perl. A plethora of other modules can be found on the Comprehensive Perl Archive Network, CPAN. See Appendix B, *Perl Links*, on page 85 for a list of URLs.

🔁 perlmodlib.
   perldoc *module* will provide the documentation for the named module.

Modules marked with an asterisk have submodules that have been omitted from the list.

AnyDBM_File
   Provides a framework for multiple DBM files.

Attribute::Handlers*
   Allows for a simpler definition of attribute handlers.

AutoLoader
   Load functions only on demand.

AutoSplit   Split a package for autoloading.

B*   Implements byte compilation, a Perl to C translator, and other interesting things. To be used with the O package. See also the section "Compiler Backends" on page 72.

Benchmark   Benchmarks running times of code.

ByteLoader
   Loads byte compiler Perl code.

Carp*   Warns of errors.

CGI*	Provides Common Gateway Interface (CGI) Classes.
Class::ISA	
	Investigates the search path for a class's IS-A tree.
Class::Struct	
	Declares struct-like data types as Perl classes.
Config	Provides access to Perl configuration information.
CPAN*	Queries, downloads and builds Perl modules from CPAN sites.
Cwd	Gets the pathname of the current working directory.
Data::Dumper	
	Stringifies Perl data structures, suitable for both printing and **eval**.
DB	Provides a programmatic interface to the Perl debugging API.
DB_File	Provides access to Berkeley DB (database) files.
Devel*	Contans tools for development of Perl itself.
Digest*	Calculates message digests, like Digest::MD5.
DirHandle	Supplies object methods for directory handles.
Dumpvalue	Provides screen dump of Perl data.
DynaLoader	
	Dynamically loads C libraries into Perl code.
Encode*	Supplies tools to deal with character encodings like Unicode, vendor-specific, and various non-Latin-based encodings.
English	Provides verbose English names for punctuation variables.
Env	Imports environment variables as scalars or arrays.
Errno	Imports names for system errors.
Exporter*	Implements default import method for modules.
ExtUtils*	Assists in the development and maintenance of Perl and Perl extension modules.
Fatal	Replaces functions with equivalents that **die** on failure.
Fcntl	Loads the C fcntl.h defines.

`File::Basename`
> Parses filenames.

`File::CheckTree`
> Runs many file checks on a hierarchy of files.

`File::Compare`
> Compares files or filehandles.

`File::Copy`
> Copies files or filehandles.

`File::DosGlob`
> Provides MS-DOS-like globbing (with extensions).

`File::Find`
> Traverses a hierarchy of files.

`File::Glob`
> Provides access to the BSD **glob** routine.

`File::Path`
> Creates or removes a series of directories.

`File::Spec`*
> Portably performs operations on filenames.

`File::stat`
> Provides a by name interface to the **stat** functions.

`File::Temp`
> Ensures safe handling of temporary files.

`FileCache` Keeps more files open than the system permits.

`FileHandle`
> Supplies object methods for filehandles.

`Filter::Simple`
> Provides simple tools for source filtering.

`Filter::Util::Call`
> Provides tools for source filtering.

`FindBin` Locates the directory of the Perl script.

`GDBM_File` Provides access to the GNU gdbm library.

`Getopt::Long`
> Provides extensive tools to handle command-line options. Suits all needs.

`Getopt::Std`

Provides simple tools to handle command-line options.

`Hash::Util`

Contains general-utility hash subroutines.

`I18N::Collate`

Compares 8-bit scalar data according to the current locale.

`I18N::Langinfo`

Queries locale information.

`I18N::LangTags`

Provides functions for dealing with RFC 3066-style language tags.

`I18N::LangTags::List`

Provides tags and names for human languages.

`IO*`   Provides various modules for object-oriented I/O.

`IPC::Msg`   Provides an interface to System V Message IPC.

`IPC::Open2`

Opens a pipe to a process for both reading and writing.

`IPC::Open3`

Opens a pipe to a process for reading, writing, and error handling.

`IPC::Semaphore`

Provides an interface to System V semaphores.

`IPC::SysV` The System V IPC object class.

`List::Util`

Contains general-utility list subroutines.

`Locale*`   Contains modules to support locales.

`Math::BigFloat*`

Enables arbitrary length float math package.

`Math::BigInt*`

Enables arbitrary size integer math package.

`Math::BigRat`

Enables arbitrary size rational numbers.

`Math::Complex`

>Contains functions for complex numbers.

`Math::Trig`

>Contains trigonometric functions.

`Memoize`   Makes functions faster by trading space for time.

`MIME::Base64`

>Enables encoding and decoding of base64 strings.

`MIME::QuotedPrint`

>Enables encoding and decoding of quoted-printable strings.

`NDBM_File` **tie**d access to NDBM files.

`Net*`   Modules for general networking. Includes network clients for FTP, SMTP, POP3 and SMTP.

`Net::hostent`

>Provides access by name to **gethostent** and friends.

`Net::netent`

>Provides access by name to **getnetent** and friends.

`Net::protoent`

>Provides access by name to **getprotoent** and friends.

`Net::servent`

>Provides access by name to **getservent** and friends.

`NEXT`   Provides a pseudo-class `NEXT` that allows method redispatch.

`O*`   The generic interface to Perl Compiler backends. See also the section "Compiler Backends" on page 72.

`Opcode`   Disables named opcodes when compiling Perl code.

`PerlIO*`   Contains modules for the PerlIO I/O layers.

`PerlIO::encoding`

>Support for encoding layers.

`PerlIO::Scalar`

>Support module for in-memory I/O.

`Pod*`   Contains modules to deal with Plain Old Documentation (POD) files. This includes parsers, and converters to HTML and LaTeX.

Pod::Usage

> Prints a usage message from embedded POD documentation.

POSIX   Provides an interface to IEEE Std 1003.1, POSIX.

Safe   Compiles and executes code in restricted compartments.

Scalar::Util

> Contains general-utility scalar subroutines.

SDBM_File **tie**d access to sdbm files.

Search::Dict

> Searches for keys in dictionary files.

SelectSaver

> Saves and restores a selected filehandle.

SelfLoader

> Load functions only on demand.

Shell   Runs shell commands transparently within Perl.

Socket   Loads the C socket.h defines and structure manipulators.

Storable   Provides persistency for Perl data structures.

Switch   Implements a Perl6-style switch statement.

Symbol   Manipulates Perl symbols and their names.

Sys::Hostname

> Determines the name of this system.

Sys::Syslog

> Provides an interface to the Unix *syslog* calls.

Term::ANSIColor

> Enables color screen output using escape sequences.

Term::Cap Provides an interface to the Unix *termcap* database.

Term::Complete

> Enables word completion for terminal input.

Term::ReadLine

> Provides an interface to various readline packages.

Test*   Provides a simple framework for writing test scripts.

`Text::Abbrev`
> Creates an abbreviation table from a list.

`Text::Balanced`
> Extracts delimited text sequences from strings.

`Text::ParseWords`
> Parses text into a list of tokens.

`Text::Soundex`
> Implements Donald Knuth's Soundex Algorithm.

`Text::Tabs`
> Expands and unexpands tabs.

`Text::Wrap`
> Enables line wrapping to form simple paragraphs.

`Thread*` Implements old style Perl threads. Obsolete. Use the **threads** pragma (page 70) instead.

`Tie::Array`
> Provides base class definitions for **tie**d arrays.

`Tie::File` Accesses the lines of a disk file via a Perl array.

`Tie::Handle`
> Provides base class definitions for **tie**d filehandles.

`Tie::Hash` Provides base class definitions for **tie**d hashes.

`Tie::Memoize`
> Adds data to a hash when needed.

`Tie::RefHash`
> Provides base classes for **tie**d hashes with references as keys.

`Tie::Scalar`
> Provides base class definitions for **tie**d scalars.

`Tie::SubstrHash`
> Enables fixed table-size, fixed key-length hashing.

`Time::gmtime`
> Provides access by name to **gmtime**.

`Time::HiRes`
> Contains high resolution alarm, sleep, gettimeofday, and interval timers.

Time::Local
    Efficiently computes time from local and GMT time.

Time::localtime
    Provides access by name to **localtime**.

Time::tm   Provides an internal object for `Time::gmtime` and `Time::localtime`.

Unicode::Collate
    Supports Unicode collation algorithms.

Unicode::Normalize
    Supports Unicode normalization forms.

Unicode::UCD
    Provides access to the Unicode Character Database.

UNIVERSAL Contains the base class for *all* classes.

User::grent
    Access by name to **getgrent** and friends.

User::pwent
    Access by name to **getpwent** and friends.

XSLoader   Dynamically loads C libraries into Perl code.

Appendix B:
Perl Links

http://www.perl.com/
> The home of Perl.

http://www.perl.org/
> Perl advocacy services.

http://www.pm.org/
> The home of the Perl Mongers, the de facto Perl user group.

http://perl-foundation.org/
> The Perl Foundation.

http://www.perlmonks.org
> On-line community of Perl users and information.

http://yetanother.org
> Non-profit organization for collaborative efforts in Computer Science. Parent to The Perl Foundation, Perl Mongers, and Perl Monks

http://www.cpan.org/
> Comprehensive Perl Archive Network, CPAN.

http://search.cpan.org/
> CPAN search engine.

http://news.perl.org/
> The Perl News site.

http://lists.perl.org/
> A huge collection of Perl-related mailing lists.

http://use.perl.org/
> A Perl Community news and discussion site.

http://reference.perl.com/
> A nice collection of Perl resources.

http://bugs.perl.org/
> The Perl bug database.

http://history.perl.org/
> Home of CPAST and the Perl Timeline.

http://www.squirrel.nl/perlref.html
> Home of the *Perl Pocket Reference* in all its incarnations.

http://www.squirrel.nl/people/jvromans/
> The author's home.

http://www.tpj.com/
> The Perl Journal.

http://www.theperlreview.com/
> The Perl Review.

Index